FALLSCHIRMJÄGER: PORTRAITS OF GERMAN PARATROOPS IN COMBAT

Also by Branislav Radovic
German Helmets of the Second World War (*two volumes*)
German Camouflaged Helmets of the Second World War (*two volumes*)

By Michael Haselgrove and Branislav Radovic
Helmets of the First World War: Germany, Britain & their Allies
The History of the Steel Helmet in the First World War (*two volumes*)

FALLSCHIRMJÄGER

PORTRAITS OF GERMAN PARATROOPS IN COMBAT

Branislav Radovic

Schiffer Military History
Atglen, PA

Book design by Robert Biondi and Branislav Radovic.

Library of Congress Catalog Number: 2006926227.

Printed in China.
ISBN: 0-7643-2565-5

Published by Schiffer Publishing Ltd.
4880 Lower Valley Road
Atglen, PA 19310
Phone: (610) 593-1777
FAX: (610) 593-2002
E-mail: Info@schifferbooks.com.
Visit our web site at: www.schifferbooks.com
Please write for a free catalog.
This book may be purchased from the publisher.
Please include $3.95 postage.
Try your bookstore first.

In Europe, Schiffer books are distributed by:
Bushwood Books
6 Marksbury Ave.
Kew Gardens, Surrey TW9 4JF
England
Phone: 44 (0)20 8392-8585
FAX: 44 (0)20 8392-9876
E-mail: info@bushwoodbooks.co.uk
www.bushwoodbooks.co.uk
Free postage in the UK. Europe: air mail at cost.
Try your bookstore first.

INTRODUCTION

How many times have we military enthusiasts flicked eagerly through a new book on a subject close to our hearts and found that though the text may be entertaining, informative and even enlightening, the images have all been seen and published many times before.

Speaking from personal experience, the images in books are often my main reason for buying it. I scour the pages looking for fresh images that might give further insight into the world of conflict, and as a collector, to illustrate uniforms, equipment and the combinations worn in various battles and campaigns.

And so it was with pleasant surprise, during a visit to the Bundesarchiv in Koblenz, Germany, that I came across many previously unseen and, indeed, unpublished photographs of the German armed forces of World War II. A surprisingly large portion of these photographs were of fallschirm units in Italy, Russia and Normandy. My reasoning was that if I would like a book of largely unseen Fallschirmjäger photographs, others might also.

Few of the Bundesarchiv's World War II images are captioned. In my captions, I have identified the images geographically, either where the Bundesarchiv or I believe them to be. If any reader has positive proof for any, I would be very interested to hear.

Although the images were taken by professional photographers, they vary in quality but are nonetheless included due to content. One of the interesting facts that emerges from the images is the mix of combat equipment and clothing. Men within the same units can be seen wearing early non-camouflaged jump smocks with later camouflaged helmet covers and vice versa.

The more images we see, the more likely we are to understand. With a broader choice of images, issues like the reported problem of the failure of the Model 38 liner system becomes clearer. I have also observed the apparent popularity of pipe-smoking within the Fallschirmjäger community.

These images exude an air of confidence, and the likelihood of victory, keeping the "home fires burning" back home and reassuring the German people that the world was safe in their competent hands.

This volume contains mid-war images from North Africa, Italy, Russia and France. The author plans to produce a subsequent book of World War II Fallschirmjäger images from other times and places.

He is especially indebted to Martina Caspers of the photographic department at the Bundesarchiv for all her help, and to Bob Biondi at Schiffer Publishing for his enthusiasm.

Greece/Crete, 1943. These men appear to be about to board a Junkers Ju 52 and are wearing quite a mixed array of equipment. The cloth helmet covers are the early clip-on olive green type. Their splinter pattern camouflage jump smocks are the mid-war variety and the parachutes are the later pattern RZ20 with quick-release straps. The man in the centre wears the side lacing jump boots; his comrades the more common front lacing. Note how the man on the left (presumably a member of a machinegun team) has wrapped a spare ammunition belt around his neck and secured it in place by his belt, which also supports a 250 round MG34/42 magazine, water bottle and Luger P.08 pistol. Note also the use of Fallschirmjäger gauntlets, binoculars, kneepads and trench torch. The equipment and caption might suggest this photograph was taken immediately prior to the operation on the Greek island of Leros.

Greece/Crete, 1943. This photograph illustrates the widespread practice of holding the static line between the teeth when enplaning.

Greece/Crete, 1943. Another Fallschirmjäger hauls himself up into the Ju 52. Note the 2nd pattern plain olive green step-in smock, front lacing boots and kneepads. Also note the clearly defined thigh pocket for the gravity knife, and the indented heel often seen on paratroop jump boots.

Greece/Crete, 1943. A close up shot of a man wearing the plain olive green clip-on cloth helmet cover with seam to the front. Clearly shown is his 2nd pattern plain olive green jump smock, the early pattern blue-grey ammunition bandolier for his Mauser 98K rifle and the quick-release mechanism on his RZ20 parachute harness.

Training. Although uncaptioned, this and the following three photographs are probably mid-war period. Note the matte finished M38 single insignia helmets and the RZ20 parachutes. They almost all wear the early 2nd pattern plain olive green step-in smocks, kneepads, gauntlets and front lacing boots. The man on the far left appears to be wearing the Fallschirmjäger rubber overshoes.

Training. A good illustration of the required stance at the door of the aircraft prior to jumping.

Training. Upward view of the open camouflaged parachute.

Training. A Fallschirmjäger floats down holding what appears to be his MP40.

Italy 1943. Training. Note the Oberleutnant flight clothing rank insignia and dummy MP40.

Training. This Unteroffizier is wearing the second pattern step-in smock.

France, 1943. Training/publicity. This and the following two images show men wearing splinter pattern jump smocks and drawstring helmet cover. Note the magnetic antitank shaped charge and Teller Mine 35.

Russia, March 1943. All three men appear to be wearing the plain second pattern jump smock. Note the MG spares pouches and plain clip-on cloth cover over a white-painted M38 helmet.

Russia (near Kironograd), December 1943. This man is wearing the grey-to-white padded reversible parka and plain clip-on helmet cover.

Russia. This Feldgendarme is wearing the reversible parka and quilted over-trousers; around his neck is the Feldgendarmerie gorget.

Russia. The man on the left is wearing a splinter-pattern-to-white padded parka with what appears to be army camouflage clothing rank insignia. His comrade, with the parka reversed to white, watches as he paints his M38 helmet white. Also note the practice of painting binoculars and other field equipment in camouflage whitewash.

Russia, March 1943. This man is wearing a white-painted M38 helmet daubed with mud, a second pattern plain jump smock with added provision for flares or rifle grenades. Around his neck is the first pattern blue-grey bandolier.

Russia, 1943. An interesting photograph of a white-painted M38 helmet with curious chinstrap arrangement, possibly due to missing snap-fastenings or an overlong chinstrap.

Russia, March 1943. The man on the left is wearing a splinter pattern clip-on cloth cover over his white-painted M38 helmet and a second pattern plain jump smock. Note his comrade has the plain clip-on cloth cover and is wearing a silk neckerchief, popular with the Fallschirm troops.

Russia. This man is wearing Feldwebel rank insignia on his second pattern smock. His chinstrap is stretched over his M38 helmet. Note also the subdued belt buckle.

Russia. (Top) This machinegunner with MG42 is wearing a heavily textured camouflaged M38 helmet and second pattern jump smock.

Russia. (Bottom) This member of 75mm antitank gun crew is wearing the fliegerbluse with Obergefreiter collar rank. His well-used M38 helmet has been whitewashed leaving the Luftwaffe "adler" insignia visible.

Tunisia, 1943. The belts of machinegun ammunition would suggest this young Fallschirmjäger was a member of a machinegun crew. He is wearing a third pattern splinter camouflage jump smock with what appears to be a splinter pattern clip-on helmet cover. Also note that he is carrying a Walther P38 pistol.

Tunisia, 1943 These men are examining a captured Thompson submachinegun. The man on the left is wearing the third pattern splinter jump smock and plain clip-on helmet cover. His comrade has a mud-daubed helmet and second pattern plain jump smock.

Although not captioned, this photograph was possibly taken in North Africa. The men are both wearing splinter pattern clip-on cloth covers over their tan-camouflaged M38 helmets. Note the partially missing cloth foliage band on the helmet at right. The man on the left has a second pattern plain jump smock while his comrade has the later splinter pattern version.

Italy (possibly near Monte Cassino). This Feldwebel is wearing the second pattern plain step-in smock over his fliegerbluse. His over-painted tan-camouflaged helmet was originally the earlier Model 37, as can be seen from the hole for the liner band attachment and slot for the carbine clip chinstrap, but then converted to take the M38 liner with spanner bolts.

Leros, Greece 1943. This Fallschirmjäger has a machinegun ammunition belt and blue-grey rifle ammunition bandolier over his splinter pattern camouflage smock.

Leros, Greece 1943. The man on the left is wearing an early twin-insignia M38 helmet. The officer, in the centre, is wearing a bleached splinter camouflage pattern visored field cap, with metal "adler" insignia and cloth roundel, and is sporting the metal Deutsches Kreuz on the breast pocket of his tropical tunic. The man on the right is wearing the plain second pattern jump smock and splinter pattern clip-on cloth helmet cover, with a version of a splinter pattern bandolier which holds rifle clips held with splinter pattern camouflaged tabs. Both men are sitting on what appears to be a captured British BSA motorcycle.

Sicily, 1943. This man appears to be wearing the long-sleeved Luftwaffe tropical shirt and trousers.

Italy, 1943/44 (Probably Gran Sasso Mussolini rescue). This Obergefreiter is wearing a heavily textured tan-camouflaged M38 helmet. Note the missing spanner bolt, indicative of the common fault with this liner system.

Gran Sasso, Italy September 1943. The man in the centre is wearing the drawstring splinter pattern cloth helmet cover. Around his neck are tinted flight goggles (presumably useful in snow) and a blue-grey rifle ammunition bandolier. Note the long leather paratroop gloves.

Gran Sasso, Italy September 1943. Taken at the foot of the cable car this photograph shows General Kurt Student in conversation with officers and civilians. In the foreground, on the tan-camouflaged Zündapp motorcycle combination, sits the driver who is wearing a second pattern plain step-in smock over Luftwaffe tropical trousers as well as a drawstring splinter pattern helmet cover while his comrade wears a tan camouflaged version of the helmet.

Italy. Possibly training for the Gran Sasso operation. The side panel of the DFS 230 glider has been lifted to reveal the seating arrangement. Here we can see plain smocks and splinter pattern smocks over their Fallschirmjäger trousers. Note the front-lacing jump boots with grooves in the heel.

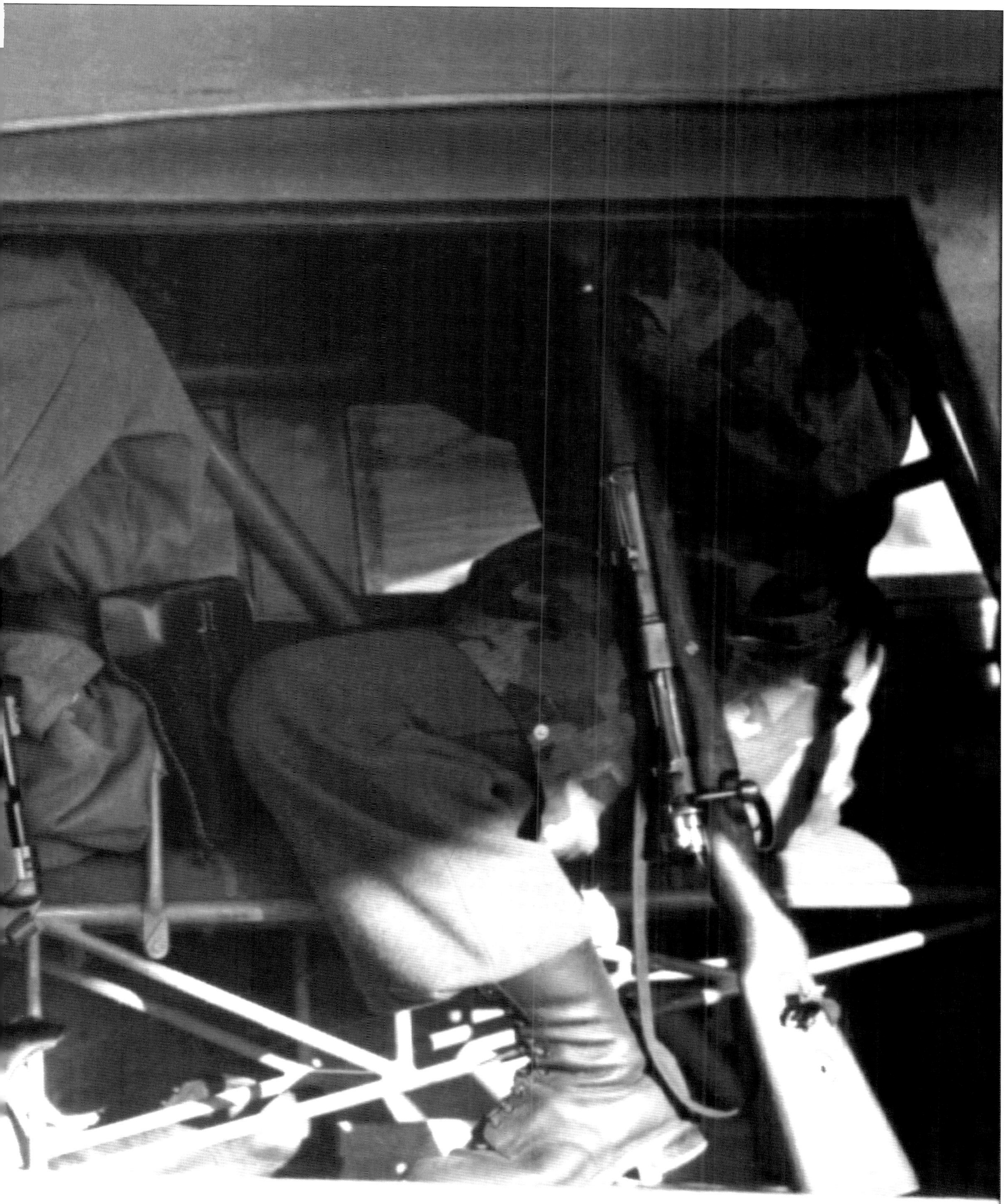

Italy. Another view of men boarding the DFS 230 glider.

Monte Cassino, Italy. This wounded, bespectacled Feldwebel is wearing the 3rd pattern splinter jump smock over his fliegerbluse. He carries a camera around his neck, which could indicate a Kriegsberichter (war correspondent). Pipe smoking seemed to be popular amongst Fallschirmjäger.

Italy, 1944. This Kriegsberichter cine photographer is wearing a tan-camouflaged M38 helmet and splinter pattern jump smock. His pipe smoking comrade is wearing a clip-on cloth cover over his tan-camouflaged M38 helmet and appears to be holding a Panzerfaust Kleine 30.

Northern Italy, 1943/44. (Top) This man is wearing a splinter pattern jump smock. His camouflaged helmet is missing the right-hand spanner bolt.

Northern Italy, 1943/44. (Bottom) A rear view of the same man, showing the metal-shod alpine boots.

Possibly Italy, 1943/44. The man on the left has a camouflage painted M38 helmet, which still shows traces of the previous season's snow camouflage. Both their netting covers are the regulation type with face veils and the man on the right has secured his with a strip from a rubber inner tube. They both wear 2nd pattern plain step-in smocks.

This mud-splattered Fallschirmjäger pauses for a damp smoke.

Italy (Top) This Fallschirmjäger is wearing what appears to be an Italian-made tan smock with horizontal breast pockets. His tan camouflaged M38 helmet has lost some of the spanner bolts and is held onto the liner with wire.

Italy (Bottom) The man on the left has tied string around his tan camouflaged helmet in order to attach foliage.

A clear shot of the textured tan camouflage on an M38 helmet.

A clear shot of the textured tan camouflage on an M38 helmet.

Captioned as near Monte Cassino, Italy, but possibly Russia. Probably the winter of 1943/44. These men are wearing reversible padded parkas, quilted and plain. Note the application of mud to the helmet.

Monte Cassino, Italy. This well camouflaged Fallschirmjäger has used the local flora inserted into his helmet and smock to blend into the landscape.

Italy, 1943. In ambush, a Model 41 Flammenwerfer.

Italy, September 1943. A twin mounted MG34. The gunner is wearing a tan camouflaged M38 helmet with regulation string netting cover with face veil and aircrew tinted goggles. He is wearing a four pocket tropical tunic with Eisernes Kreuz 1st Class pinned to his pocket.

Italy, 1943/44. This man has inserted foliage into his splinter pattern clip-on cloth helmet cover. He is wearing the 3rd pattern splinter jump smock.

Italy 1943/44. A clear shot of newly issued single insignia M38 helmets in the dark matte factory finish. They are wearing the 3rd pattern splinter jump smock.

Near Monte Cassino, Italy. A gunner sets up his MG42 on its Lafette 42 tripod stand. He is wearing the quilted reversible padded parka.

Italy, 1944. (Top) The M38 and the M42 helmets compared.

Italy, 1943/44. (Bottom) A detailed view of the splinter pattern clip-on helmet cover and smock.

Italy 1944. A Feldwebel with flight rank insignia on his 2nd pattern plain step-in smock. His M38 helmet has a smooth tan camouflage finish.

Italy 1944. A veteran of the invasion of Crete wearing the campaign cufftitle on his Unteroffizier fliegerbluse at a forward observation post overlooking the Nettuno countryside. His helmet has a plain clip-on cloth cover. Also note the metal Fallschirmjäger badge pinned to his left breast.

Italy 1944. This Feldwebel is wearing his Eisernes Kreuz 1st Class and whistle cord on his Luftwaffe tropical tunic. His plain clip-on helmet cover is worn with the rear seam to the front.

Italy 1944. Two men on a Zündapp motorcycle.

Italy 1944. A young Fallschirmjäger with 3rd pattern splinter jump smock, MP40 and ammunition pouches.

Italy 1944. Seen in a previous photograph, this Crete veteran uses the binocular rangefinder covered in string netting camouflage.

Nettuno, Italy 1943. Pausing for a smoke, this man is wearing a plain 2nd pattern jump smock and blue-grey rifle ammunition bandolier.

Nettuno, Italy 1943. Again we see the plain 2nd pattern jump smock being worn by this pipe-smoker. His M38 helmet has the plain clip-on cover and over his shoulder hangs a grenade bag.

Nettuno, Italy 1943. Clutching his bottle of wine, this Fallschirmjäger is wearing the plain 2nd pattern smock and over his helmet the regulation string net.

Nettuno, Italy 1943. Here we see the plain and splinter pattern smocks. Note the man on the left is wearing early side lacing jump boots. His comrade's M38 helmet is camouflaged in tan.

Nettuno, Italy 1943. The ubiquitous pipe.

Nettuno, Italy 1943. A nice clear shot of a snow camouflaged M38 helmet overpainted in tan. The man on the right wears the splinter drawstring cloth cover. Also note the plastic zippers on the plain smock.

Nettuno, Italy 1943. Possibly shown on a previous photograph, this Fallschirmjäger with tan camouflaged M38 helmet has had to use wire to attach his helmet to the liner, probably because the spanner bolt(s) had sheared. He carries a blanket, an MP40 with ammunition pouches, a map case and a flare pistol.

Italy, 1943/44. A slightly wounded Fallschirmjäger with 3rd pattern splinter jump smock and plain clip-on cloth helmet cover.

Nettuno, Italy 1943/44. Officers/NCOs discuss tactics. The man on the left is wearing a theatre-made drawstring cloth cover from what appears to be Italian camouflage material. The man on the right wears his splinter pattern clip-on cover over a white camouflaged helmet.

Italy, 1943/44. Men on the Italian invasion front pause for a smoke. All wear the plain 2nd pattern jump smock. Note the loose chinstrap indicating the seemingly common failure of the liner system attachment.

Nettuno, Italy 1943. (Top) The officers' side cap and M43 cap being worn.

Nettuno, Italy 1943/44. (Bottom) This Fallschirmjäger scans the sky. His M38 helmet has a smooth tan finish. Note the woollen gloves and M43 cap tucked into his splinter pattern smock.

Italy, 1943/44. This man's chinstrap has been tied together. Note the flare pistol tucked into his 3rd pattern splinter jump smock.

Italy, 1943/44. Our Fallschirmjäger with broken chinstrap from a previous photograph sports a captured British Bren gun.

Italy, 1943/44. A convoy of Fallschirmjäger on BMW motorcycles and Sd.Kfz.231 armoured cars heads south along the coast road from Rome towards the invasion front. Note the early M38 helmet with national shield insignia.

Italy, 1943/44. A typical group of Fallschirmjäger facing the Allied invasion of Italy. They all wear the plain 2nd pattern jump smock. Note that the man on the end is wearing a M35/42 helmet rather than the M38.

Italy, 1943/44. Wearing a plain 2nd pattern jump smock, blue-grey rifle ammunition bandolier and stick grenades, this Fallschirmjäger scans the horizon. His M38 helmet is painted tan with darker patches and is covered in the Fallschirmjäger issue netting cover.

Monte Cassino, Italy 1943. A Ritterkreuz winner with a plain 2nd pattern jump smock and tan painted M38 helmet.

Monte Cassino, Italy 1943. Looking through a binocular rangefinder this soldier has used a captured British netting cover for his M38 helmet.

Italy, 1943/44. This machinegunner takes a nap in his slit trench. His M38 helmet has all but lost its tan camouflage.

Nettuno, Italy, 1943. This man is wearing a splinter pattern jump smock. His M38 helmet has been bound in wire with foliage attached.

Possibly Italy. This Oberfeldwebel is wearing the Eisernes Kreuz 2nd Class ribbon on his fliegerbluse. His helmet appears to be painted tan. Note the plaited whistle lanyard.

Italy. Laying telephone lines, this Fallschirmjäger is wearing Luftwaffe tropical trousers and shirt. His helmet is painted tan

Crete, Greece 1941. A company bugler, pictured here outside the Sturmregiment HQ in Chania, is wearing the plain 2nd pattern jump smock with Unteroffizier flight clothing insignia and splinter pattern clip-on cloth helmet cover.

Possibly Italy. This Fallschirmjäger is wearing a bread bag strap over his helmet to secure the splinter pattern drawstring cover. Note the blue-grey rifle ammunition bandolier worn over the 3rd pattern jump smock.

Rome, Italy 1943. Following the Italian decision to change sides after the invasion, Fallschirmjäger take up defensive positions and oversee the surrender of Italian weapons and equipment. Note the universal use of Luftwaffe tropical trousers under splinter pattern jump smocks.

Italy, 1943/44. Italian paratroopers of the Nembo Division with German Fallschirmjäger. Note the Beretta 38a machine pistol ammunition magazine and grenade pouches. Most of the Italians are wearing German 3rd pattern splinter smocks. One paratrooper, wearing a torque under his helmet is wearing an Italian camouflaged type. Another shown eating is wearing what appears to be a plain Italian smock and has threaded wire through the vent holes of his M33 helmet for the attachment of foliage. Note the use of British and German netting covers alongside the Italian cloth helmet cover. The man fourth from the left appears to be wearing an MVSN Italian fighting knife next to his Beretta pistol. The presence of British netting covers would suggest the location to be the Nettuno invasion area.

Monte Cassino, Italy 1943. Good v ews of the use of British camouflage helmet netting.

Northern Italy, 1943/44. An example of a helmet with tan camouflage applied over a previous white scheme.

Italy, 1943. Fallschirmjäger of the Sturmregiment pay their last respects to fallen comrades. The Leutnant is wearing an M43 cap with a metal shooting star (symbol of the Sturmregiment) and an Italian, privately-made tan smock. The Feldwebel is wearing a hastily made helmet cover of seemingly odd pieces of splinter pattern camouflage material.

Monte Cassino, Italy 1943. Cassino commander Hauptmann Rennecke wearing the officers' side cap and SS camouflaged smock, briefs men sheltering in the ruins of the monastery after it was bombed by Allied aircraft. Second from the left is Oberleutnant Renisch CO of 2nd company 1st Fallschirm Regiment who wears some sort of private-purchase or even Italian tunic. Note also that the man wearing an M35/42 helmet and splinter pattern armoured crew wrap around tunic.

Rome, Italy 1943. This Fallschirmjäger, wearing the 3rd pattern jump smock has a grenade sack and blue-grey rifle ammunition bandolier slung around his neck. His plain M38 helmet has an issue string netting cover attached.

Rome, Italy 1943. These men are wearing typical clothing for the period. They stand amid surrendered Italian arms and equipment in 3rd pattern splinter jump smocks over Luftwaffe tropical trousers. Their helmets are covered with issue string netting covers. What is not typical is the use of the 1st pattern FG42 automatic rifle specifically designed for Fallschirmjäger troops. Note the splinter pattern FG42 ammunition bandolier.

Italy, 1943/44. This Feldwebel leads a patrol through the snow and looks suitably heroic for the Kriegsberichter and his camera. He is wearing the 3rd pattern splinter camouflaged jump smock and padded leather mittens with trigger finger allowing him to use his MP40. His M38 helmet is plain and possibly newly issued. His men wear a variety of equipment, 2nd and 3rd pattern smocks, tan camouflaged and plain M38 helmets. Also note the embroidered cloth cross patch on his left forearm.

Italy, 1943/44. A gooc shot of the front lacing jump boots.

Italy, 1943. The long-sleeved Luftwaffe tropical shirt worn with Unteroffizier shoulderboards. This Fallschirmjäger has a tan camouflaged M38 helmet.

Italy, June/July 1944. Note this man's M38 helmet has been heavily textured with sand/soil and paint, over which has been placed wire for the attachment of foliage.

Probably Italy 1943/44. This man's helmet appears to have been painted with a light camouflage colour, then overpainted again in subtle darker mottled colours.

Dated 1944, probably Italy. This man, apparently a member of a machinegun crew, has spare ammunition belts draped around his shoulders over his long-sleeved tropical shirt with epaulettes. His helmet has the splinter pattern clip-on cloth cover.

Dated 1944, possibly Rome. At least one of these Fallschirmjäger is wearing an early style, twin insignia M38 helmet with sliding chinstrap. The netting covers are the type produced specifically for Fallschirmjäger. Note the rifle grenade launcher carried by the man at centre. Also of interest is the blurred Fallschirmjäger with a clip-on cloth cover over his standard M35/42 helmet (this man can be seen in greater detail several pages further on).

Monte Cassino, Italy, but possibly Russia. This Fallschirmjäger MG42 gunner is wearing the quilted reversible parka and a thinly whitewashed M38 helmet.

Gran Sasso, Italy 1943. (Top) A machinegunner with his MG34, splinter pattern smock and tan camouflaged helmet. Note the damaged stock.

Italy, 1944. (Bottom) This MG42 crew are wearing the regulation string netting covers over their M38 helmets. The man on the left has Luftwaffe tropical trousers while his comrade wears Fallschirmjäger jump trousers. Both wear front lacing boots.

Dated 1944, possibly Rome. This photograph clearly shows an Unteroffizier using a clip-on cloth cover for the M38 to cover a standard M35/42 helmet. His pipe smoking comrade is wearing what seems to be an Italian-made tropical tunic and a well-worn tan camouflaged M38 helmet.

Russia. A splinter pattern clip-on cloth cover being worn over a camouflaged M38 helmet and plain 2nd pattern jump smock. Note the stick grenades tucked into his belt.

Russia. This MG34 gunner, festooned with extra ammunition belts is wearing a plain 2nd pattern smock. Note the gas cape and Luger pistol on a lanyard tucked into his pocket.

Uncaptioned but probably Italy, 1944. He wears a non-regulation cloth helmet cover made from either parachute material or more likely Italian camouflage over which is placed a homemade foliage strap with three or four hooks attached. His jump smock is the plain 2nd pattern.

Normandy, 1944. Fallschirmjäger Feldpolizei reconnoitre the area, possibly looking for dispersed U.S. paratroopers, some riding a BMW motorcycle combination. They all wear a mixture of plain and camouflaged smocks. Note the regulation string netting helmet covers and the varied methods of attaching wire, rubber inner tube and chicken wire.

Captioned as Holland but more likely to be Normandy, 1944. A rare but previously published photograph of a Fallschirmjäger sturmgeschütz commander in his turret. Note the method of wearing headphones over the M38 helmet allowing him to hear the radio and extraneous sounds at the same time.

Normandy, 1944. This young Fallschirmjäger is wearing a cage of chicken wire stiffened with heavy gauge wire over his helmet. His smock is the later splinter pattern model.

Normandy, 1944. A Fallschirmjäger Leutnant with a battered peaked service cap accepts a light. He wears the 3rd pattern splinter jump smock.

Normandy, 1944. This Oberleutnant is wearing a splinter camouflaged clip-on helmet cover and a plain 2nd pattern jump smock.

Normandy, 1944. A dug-in Fallschirmjäger takes aim with his 1st pattern FG42 automatic rifle. His helmet is covered with the regulation string netting, held in place by a rubber tyre inner tube.

Normandy, 1944. An interesting photograph of a variation to the usual splinter pattern drawstring helmet cover. The foliage band is thinner and nearer to the rim than the regulation type suggesting a theatre-made example. Also note the egg grenades hanging from his belt.

Normandy, 1944. Gaunt and battle-weary Fallschirmjäger. The standing figure has a well-worn string netting cover on his helmet and his jump smock is the late war 3rd pattern tan/water camouflage.

Normandy, 1944. This Fallschirmjäger has attached a variety of foliage to his helmet. He carries a Panzerfaust 30 on his shoulder.

Normandy, 1944. In the bocage, overlooking a field, this man wears a brightly camouflaged M42 helmet, probably tan with green splashes. His smock is the later tan/water type.

Normandy, 1944. This Fallschirmjäger sports a typical "Normandy" style camouflage helmet of tan oversprayed with brown and green patches. His jump smock is the plain 2nd pattern variety.

Normandy, 1944. A motorcyclist takes a brief rest. His M38 helmet is painted with darker stripes, leaving some of the original finish and "adler" insignia. Note the aircrew goggles and rubberised motorcyclists' coat.

Normandy, 1944. A Fallschirmjäger anti-aircraft gunner with well-worn drawstring splinter pattern cloth cover. Note the embroidered other ranks' Luftwaffe "adler" sewn onto his 3rd pattern camouflaged jump smock.

Normandy, 1944. A young man who has obviously been in the field for some time. His drawstring splinter pattern cloth helmet cover has his name on the foliage tape.

Normandy, 1944. Officers confer in the bocage. The Leutnant's helmet on the left has dark patches of paint over a lighter tan base with wire attached which has moved revealing the lighter base colour. Note the different types of camouflage smock being worn, splinter and tan/water.

Normandy, 1944. A nice example of a tan camouflaged M38 helmet with added chicken wire. Note the large open weave of the wire and generally, the variation of chicken wire types pictured throughout the book. He also wears what appears to be a re-sewn cloth "adler" on his splinter pattern jump smock.

Normandy, 1944. This Feldwebel wears a plain helmet and a clearly defined printed splinter pattern jump smock.

Normandy, 1944. A Fallschirmjäger with a painted camouflaged helmet and what appears to be two string netting covers added.

Normandy, 1944. Men serving at the front were able to marry their sweethearts by proxy in the field. This young Panzerjäger Fallschirmjäger Leutnant is married by his commanding officer in a ceremony beside a Pak 40 and images of Hitler and Göring. Note the letter "P" on his epaulette denoting Panzerjäger. He also wears the fliegerbluse and peaked service cap.

Normandy, 1944. A close up shot of the regulation string netting helmet cover held on by rubber inner tube.

Normandy, 1944. The 3rd pattern splinter jump smock.

Normandy, 1944. A group of contemplative Fallschirmjäger, one wearing an M35/42 helmet. All have regulation string netting covers over camouflage painted helmets.

Normandy, 1944. The man without whom none of these pictures would have been possible – a Fallschirmjäger Kriegsberichter at work.

Normandy, 1944. An interesting image of a Fallschirmjäger wearing a plain 2nd pattern jump smock with added pocket to the lower left arm in splinter camouflage material. His M38 helmet has a splinter pattern clip-on cloth cover with looped baling wire added.

Budapest, 1945. Although not of the best quality, these four rare photographs show two members of SS Fallschirmjäger Battalion 600 after the storming and capture of the citadel in Budapest, Hungary by Otto Skorzeny's Kampfgruppe. Note the plain M38 helmets, the late 3rd pattern tan/water jump smocks, and the SS other ranks belt buckles. The figure in the last photo wears mountain boots with metal cleats.

Greece/Crete, 1941. Another view of the Sturmregiment's bugler outside its HQ in the old British Consulate (now Doma Hotel) in Chania.